# One Message
# One Truth

## The Prophecies of the Blessed Virgin at Fatima, Lourdes, Akita and Other Approved Apparitions.

D0729582

*Daniel Connolly*

The intended use of this book is to provide a deeper knowledge
of Roman Catholicism through one aspect of it, namely,
approved Marian apparitions.

Cover design by Lance Eberlein and Daniel Connolly.

"We are now standing in the face of the greatest historical confrontation humanity has gone through. ...I do not think that wide circles of the Christian Community realize this fully. We are now facing the final confrontation between the Church and the anti-Church, of the Gospel versus the anti-Gospel."
Karol Cardinal Wojtyla addressing the Eucharistic Congress, 1976

Dedicated to the Virgin of the Apocalypse

# Table of Contents

# Author's Note

First, I want to thank you for reading this book. I also want to say that feedback is appreciated and criticism welcome - if something important was missed it needs to be corrected for future editions. Please let me know.

At the time of this writing, April 2012, this book is (as far as I can tell), unlike other books on Marian apparitions. It presents a fresh look at something already well documented and so widely known. There is definitely no shortage of well-researched classics on this topic, yet this book presents the messages as one cohesive unit, which is unique. My aim for the reader then is to 1) provide insight that may not have been considered until now and 2) to present it in a clear and easily readable format.

Finally, I would like to extend my thanks to everyone who provided me with their knowledge and resources. It could not have been done without you. This is true not only of your insights but also of your libraries. Sometimes, information is presented to us the old fashioned way – through books – which I like.

Thank you again.

Daniel Connolly
April 2, 2012
Monday in Passion Week
onemessageonetruth@yahoo.com

# Introduction

Visions of the Blessed Virgin Mary are nothing new to the Catholic Church. In fact, Church history is filled with the stories of those granted just such a privilege. It is easy to think of these select souls as being the greatest of saints, and in many cases, as you would expect, they are. But just as often, the 'little guys' too have been granted a meeting with Heaven. San Juan Diego comes to mind for example, as do Francisco, Jacinta and their cousin Lucia. And these, of course, are not the only ones. We will look at the others here as well.

It is a fact that these glimpses of the supernatural are closely guarded by the Church. They always have been and always will. They are treated with care and, while being taken seriously, are treated judiciously. For every legitimate, verified apparition, there are many others that fall far short of the mark and the Church rules definitively against them. The hoax of Bayside for instance, comes readily to mind.

So in these pages we will be considering only those apparitions approved by the Church; those meetings with the supernatural that fit the category of 'private revelation' and are 'worthy of belief' by not contradicting or compromising the Faith in any way.

Like all Catholics, I had always known about the apparitions of Our Lady but my interest was piqued after reading an interview in *Jesus* magazine with Cardinal Ratzinger, then Prefect of the Congregation for the Doctrine of the Faith. The interview ran in the 1984, November issue, and dealt with the 'Third Secret of Fatima' and why it had not been released up to that point. The interviewer asked, "Have you read it (the 'Third Secret')?" To which Cardinal Ratzinger replied, "Yes. I have read it." The interviewer continued, "Then why has it not been released?" The Cardinal responded, "Because the things contained in this 'Third Secret' correspond to what has been announced in Scripture and has been said again and again in many other Marian apparitions..."[1] From that moment I wanted to find out more.

Our objective then, is to consider Cardinal Ratzinger's statement by looking at the messages contained in the various apparitions. These messages are public and well known and are therefore easily accessible to anyone who wants to read them. The Cardinal did not quote the Scriptural passages to which he was referring but when Sister Lucia was asked about the Secret, she

---

1 *Jesus* magazine, November 11, 1984, p.79.

said, "It is in the Gospel and the Apocalypse.  Read them!"[2]  Thus we will look to see what the 'unifying theme' is, should there be one, that links the messages together as Cardinal Ratzinger seems to imply.

---

2  Brother Michel de la Sainte Trinité, *The Whole Truth About Fatima – The Third Secret, Vol. III* (Buffalo, New York: Immaculate Heart Publications, 1990), p.763.

# Part One

# Setting the Stage
## Chapter 1

The messages of the Blessed Virgin found in approved apparitions present a simple, cohesive theme, as you would expect. And that theme is something all Catholics are familiar with: pray the rosary daily, visit the Sacraments frequently, do penance regularly, etc. These practices are integral to the spiritual life of any Catholic taking the Faith seriously and they comprise the true route needed to achieve Heaven. It is how the saints perfected their lives and how the rest of us try to.

Another aspect begins to emerge however, when the apparitions are considered from a different angle. The messages foretell increasingly dark days coming upon the Church and there is a very clear link with the Apocalypse. Not only is the theme a recurring one but the intensity of the messages also increases. The 'buzz words' generated by these apparitions include 'apostasy', 'the end times', 'Freemasonry in the Catholic Church' and 'the arrival of the Antichrist'. If you are interested in the state or fate of the Church, it would be hard to ignore the apparitions as being simply nice, pious additions to the Faith. The messages in fact, become rather frightening.

In the first chapters of Genesis we read that the heel of the Virgin will crush the head of the serpent. In the Book of Apocalypse we see that prophecy being fulfilled. And in this final book, which depicts the great struggle at the end of history, three figures come to the fore. First, we see the woman from Genesis but she is now crowned with twelve stars. She is clothed with the sun and has the moon at her feet. It is the Virgin of the Apocalypse. Second, we see the archangel Saint Michael and he, with the Virgin, casts Satan and his followers into Hell forever. Finally, we see that Satan is to war against the Church and her clergy and, for a time, will come seemingly close to destroying them.

The Blessed Virgin has appeared numerous times over the centuries because she is concerned with only one thing: the eternal life of her children. For Catholics, the fact that apparitions have happened, or might be happening, is par for the course. Sometimes, we even grow a little too accustomed to these supernatural occurrences. What we know however, is that they are given to us to serve as aids, bolster our faith and ever remind us of the 'straight and narrow'.

We do not know the specifics of how history will end, though some

1

persons have been given glimpses of the events that will usher in that time. In the Gospels, Jesus admonishes all to watch and remain vigilant. What we do know is that there is to be an apostasy within the Catholic Church and that the final battle will take place between Satan, Saint Michael the Archangel, and the Virgin of the Apocalypse.

"And a great sign appeared in heaven: A woman clothed with the sun, and the moon under her feet and on her head a crown of twelve stars."
Apocalypse 12:1

# A Woman Clothed With the Sun
## Chapter 2

Our Lady of Guadalupe
1531 – Guadalupe (Mexico City), Mexico
Visionary – San Juan Diego
Points to Consider:
  - Apocalyptic Imagery on the Tilma
  - The Virgin of the Apocalypse Triumphs Over Satan

Unlike most of the Marian apparitions which we will be considering, Guadalupe is not overly prophetic in tone. At the heart of the message however, there is a reiteration of basic, fundamental Catholic truth and this truth sets the stage for those apparitions which follow.

The truth is that only in the Catholic religion does Mary play a significant role in the course of man's daily affairs. In addition to being the Mother of God, she is also our Mother and was given to us by Jesus before He expired on the Cross. From that time forward, she has been there to assist and correct the faithful as they work out their salvation here below.

Mary is integral to the history of redemption, and in those early chapters of Genesis we see that she is the one chosen to crush the serpent. But at Guadalupe it is clear that we have come full circle. Satan is vanquished and this time it is by the "Woman clothed with the sun", the Virgin of the Apocalypse.

\*\*\*

By the early 1500's, like every other colonizing nation of Europe, the Spanish were sailing west. A main part of their agenda however, was the establishment of the Catholic religion in the New World. This was undertaken by the Franciscan missionaries who started arriving shortly thereafter in 1522.

Arriving first, the soldiers began making headway immediately.

3

Behind them lay their homeland and families, and the sound of the waves which crashed against the beach. Ahead lay dense vegetation and a harsh, humid climate. So in they went, penetrating their new home, the Central American jungle. Before long however, they would be horrified with what they would find. For they discovered a civilization steeped in human sacrifice on a massive scale.

The sacrifices took place at the apex of a stone, pyramid-like structure where the victims were held down and stretched over a flat rock while the executioner cut into their skin to remove a beating heart. These butchers were well versed in their work and could finish the job in seconds. Simply put, this new 'culture' was brutal. The heartless body was then thrown from the top of the pyramid where it would tumble and bounce until finally coming to rest on a pile of other fresh corpses.

When they arrived, the Spanish friars worked hard to end a practice so ghastly but found themselves simply overwhelmed. With the native population estimated at sixteen million, it was only through great effort that

*The miraculous and apocalyptic image of Guadalupe. The pigment is of unknown origin.*

4

conversions started to happen. Even then the number amounted to little more than a handful.

Overworked and short on supplies, the friars thought that only a miracle could turn the tide in their favor. In 1531, the "Woman clothed with the sun" did intervene to crush the dark religion and the miracle she performed would usher in the conversion of a people, the Aztec nation.

The appearances of the Blessed Virgin to Juan Diego, and his subsequent journeys to the Archbishop are famous. The Archbishop asked Juan Diego to bring him a sign so he too could believe in the visitations. During the next apparition, Juan Diego was told by the Virgin to fill his tilma (a garment made from cactus fiber), with the roses growing out of season on the December hillside. He complied and took the roses to the Archbishop. However, as Juan Diego opened his tilma, instead of the roses simply falling to the ground, a miraculous image of the Virgin was also produced. She was clothed with the sun and surrounded by stars. The moon was at her feet. It was the Virgin from the Book of Apocalypse. The sign asked for by the Archbishop had been given and it was incredible. But what happened in the subsequent years was equally incredible, perhaps even more so.

This people, steeped in ritual and mass murder, converted to the Catholic religion. What had started out as a mere trickle soon swelled into a tsunami of human deliverance and the friars were now faced with a different problem; they could barely keep up with the new demand. Within eight years of the apparitions, a staggering nine million individuals converted to Roman Catholicism. The New World, like the Old World before it, became a baptized culture infused with supernatural grace.

It is the triumph of Mary over Satan. We see it at Guadalupe but it does not end there. The difference is that after Guadalupe the tone and intensity of the messages rapidly escalates.

5

"The Church will find herself attacked by terrible assaults
from the Masonic sect."
The Blessed Virgin to Mother Mariana

# Freemasonry and the Catholic Church
## Chapter 3

Our Lady of Good Success
1628 – Quito, Ecuador
Visionary - Mother Mariana de Jesus Torres
Main Points to Consider:
  - Freemasonry is Prophesied by the Virgin
  - Extreme Duress in the Church
  - Fire Will Fall From the Sky
  - The Blessed Virgin Crushes Satan
  - A Complete Restoration is Promised

At Quito, a war is announced that will rock the twentieth century and beyond. Creating unparalleled stress in the Church, it is the war of Freemasonry and secularism against a truly Catholic life. It is a time when the voices of those who should speak out, the bishops, remain silent. Here Freemasonry is prophesied by the Virgin long before its fury is unleashed on society and the Church. And it is this ideology, according to Catholic author and former 33rd degree Mason John Salza, that has been condemned by the Catholic Church more than any other.

The prophecies of Quito announce an almost total breakdown in the Catholic spirit and this breakdown will lead to gross immorality in society causing a massive shortage of vocations. The result will be the destruction of many souls. Through the sins of impurity especially, many souls will fall. Our lives then, carry the weight of eternal consequences and it is this weight that today, vast numbers of persons completely reject. To help remedy this, Mother Mariana was asked at Quito to suffer for the Church and the salvation of souls.

\*\*\*

As a Conceptionist nun, Mother Mariana de Jesus Torres experienced many visions of the Blessed Virgin. She was also gifted with prophecy and foresaw many of the calamities which would beleaguer the Church in the latter days. One of Mother Mariana's prophecies tells us,

> Masonry, which will then be in power, will enact iniquitous laws with the objective of doing away with this Sacrament (marriage). This will make it easy for everyone to live in sin and will encourage the procreation of illegitimate children born without being incorporated into the Church. The Christian spirit will rapidly decay and the precious light of Faith will gradually be extinguished until it reaches the point that there will be a general and almost total corruption of customs. The effects of secular education will increase, which will be one reason for the dearth of priestly and religious vocations.[1]

*Freemasonry announcing a New World Order, the Novus Ordo Saeclorum.*

*Asked to suffer for the "crimes of the latter days", Mother Mariana now lies incorrupt.*

Speaking of our time, the Blessed Virgin warns that impurity will "permeate the atmosphere... Like a filthy ocean, it will run through the streets, squares and public places with an astonishing liberty." Without the grace of virginity, it will "be necessary for fire from Heaven to rain down

---

1. Marian Therese Horvat, Ph. D, *Our Lady of Good Success – Prophecies For Our Times* (Los Angeles, California: Tradition in Action, Inc., 1999), p. 46.

upon these lands in order to purify them."[2]

The Blessed Virgin tells us,

> The passions will erupt and there will be a total corruption of customs, for Satan will reign almost completely by means of the Masonic sects. They will focus particularly on the children in order to achieve this general corruption. Woe to the children of these times! ...The devil will assiduously try to destroy the Sacrament of Confession.[3]

It is true that the lines outside of the confessionals are often a little 'quiet'. This Sacrament, we seem to forget, restores to the soul the purity and innocence lost by sin. From a purely natural outlook 'confessing' is a healthy practice but Christ instituted it to increase the supernatural life in our soul. Through confession we correct our wrongs, fortify against our faults and have our guilt washed away. We also increase the grace within our soul. This is one reason why the devil puts so much effort into destroying it.

Of these latter times we are told,

> ...There will be unbridled luxury, which acting thus to entice the rest into sin, will conquer innumerable frivolous souls who will be lost. Innocence will almost no longer be found in women, nor modesty in women. In this supreme moment of need of the Church, those who should speak will fall silent.[4]

It would be tough to argue that this has not come to pass. As a society, we are living in the technologically richest period of man's history. These are certainly days of "unbridled luxury", as the Virgin tells us. We are overloaded with cell phones, the internet, television, movies and so many other conveniences, that it is more difficult than ever, often impossible, to hear the whisper of the Holy Ghost. Man relishes his advances but it is clear that the easy living they help foster puts him at odds with his supernatural calling. The 'fruits' of these advances often result in a deadening of the soul as they easily kill a spirit of penance and quell a thirst for the eternal.

One day, Jesus appeared to Mother Mariana while she prayed before

---

2. Ibid., p. 56.
3. Ibid., p. 44.
4. Ibid., p. 46.

the tabernacle. She gazed upon Him disfigured by the sufferings of Calvary and heard the voice of God the Father saying, "This punishment will be for the 20th century." At that point Mother Mariana saw three swords each with the words "I shall punish heresy, blasphemy and impurity..." written on them. When asked if she would "suffer for the people of this time?", she readily agreed that she would. The swords were then thrust into her heart and she died (She died on three different occasions, in fact.). Mother Mariana was then summoned to her judgment and given a choice. She could remain in Heaven or return and make reparation for the latter days. She chose to return.[5]

In a final apparition, Our Lord spoke to Mother Mariana about the heavy weight of Divine Justice,

> Know... that Divine Justice releases terrible chastisements on entire nations, not only for the sins of the people, but especially for those of priests and religious persons. For the latter are called, by the perfection of their state, to be the salt of the earth, the masters of truth and the deflectors of divine wrath. Straying from their divine mission, they degrade themselves in such a way that, before the eyes of God, they quicken the rigor of punishments...[6]

As predicted, the Church has few vocations today. After being decimated by a fallout rate of between eighty-five to ninety-five percent following Vatican II, the majority of religious orders now have but a few aging bodies in the ranks - with precious few young people in sight. If there is any good news in this, it would be that after experiencing an almost total demolition of her supernatural life and means of combat, the Church can only build upward once again.

At Quito, Mother Mariana was told of the absolute importance of the consecrated life,

> Woe to the world should it lack monasteries and convents! Men do not comprehend their importance, for, if they understood, they would do all in their power to multiply them... No one on the face of the earth is aware whence comes the salvation of souls, the conversion of great sinners, the end of great scourges, the fertility of the land, the end of pestilence and wars and the harmony between

---

5. Ibid., p. 27.
6. Ibid., p. 63.

nations. All this is due to the prayers that rise up from monasteries and convents.[7]

If convents and monasteries put an end to scourges, trying to make do without them is spiritual suicide. If a soul or group of nations insists on rejecting God however, little can be done to stop them. In His love, God is compelled to let the sinner exercise his free will.

The deluge of impurity warned about at Quito, so prevalent in movies, on the internet and elsewhere, is consumed with impunity, while from the majority of Catholic leaders we only hear a deafening silence. Especially sad is that it does not end there. This secular spirit and the spirit of Freemasonry foretold by the Virgin seems to have penetrated the depths of Catholic liturgical life too, where an endless stream of inanities is never far away.

To see this, all one need do is turn on YouTube to watch incoherent 'Barney Blessings', 'Clown Masses', 'Soccer Ball Masses' and the bishop of San Francisco giving the Eucharist to homosexuals in nun habits during his Mass. (Nausea will quickly follow.) The faithful then, are put in the worst of crossfires and are forced to ask questions like, "If a Catholic priest is *alter Christus*, why would he want to offer a 'Barney Blessing' instead? What exactly is a 'Barney Blessing'? One begins to wonder that if a 'Barney Blessing' is being given at Mass, is it simply better not to go? Why would we, or should we, want to take part in such a sad sacrilege?

And, as the Blessed Virgin has predicted, gone is the Church's answer to this – religious houses filled with consecrated souls dedicating themselves to the triumph of Christ through prayer and sacrifice. As the saying goes, where there is smoke there is fire so it would be tough not to conclude that "the smoke of Satan" so famously lamented by Pope Paul VI has now, seemingly, turned into a rollicking flame.

The words to Mother Mariana are not 'pretty'. We find ourselves on the front-lines of a titanic struggle in which a culture once Christian has taken on the spirit of the world and Freemasonry, and now largely rejects any supernatural motive or presence. Great is the number of those who live and die as though actions carry no consequences. We are told that "unbridled luxury" and the "sins of impurity" will be the ruin of many souls. At Quito, like Guadalupe, the Virgin promises victory over the serpent but it does not come without a price. The faithful must first be truly tested,

---

7. Ibid., p. 66.

The small number of souls who, hidden, will preserve the treasure of the Faith and practice virtue will suffer a cruel, unspeakable and prolonged martyrdom... To test this Faith and confidence of the just, there will be occasions when all will seem to be lost and paralyzed. This, then, will be the happy beginning of the complete restoration.[8]

The remedy is twofold. First, love of the Eucharist should be paramount and second, the faithful must cultivate a devotion to the Immaculate Heart of Mary. Devotion to the Immaculate Heart of course, will only lead us to her Son in the Eucharist, and the Eucharist is the bulwark which will fortify against, and make reparation for, the sins of indifference, sacrilege and other numerous abominations. It is devotion to these two treasures that will bring about a Catholic restoration and put an end to the spirit of the world and Freemasonry now infecting the Church.

The body of Mother Mariana, along with five other sisters from her convent, is incorrupt. As a testament to the truth of the apparitions and her holiness, her body has not suffered the effects of decomposition over the last four hundred years.

---

8. Ibid., p. 55.

"Times are evil in the world."
The Blessed Virgin to Catherine Laboure

# The Miraculous Medal and the Virgin of the Apocalypse
## Chapter 4

Our Lady of the Miraculous Medal
1830 – Paris, France
Visionary - Saint Catherine Laboure
Main Points to Consider:
  - Apocalyptic Imagery on the Miraculous Medal
  - Mary Converts Souls

The imagery on the Miraculous Medal is remarkable for two reasons. First, it is the same as that of chapter twelve in the Book of Apocalypse. The head of the Virgin is surrounded by a luminous crown while at her feet is the moon. Beneath her heel is, of course, Satan getting crushed. On the medal's obverse side are found the Sacred Heart of Jesus, the Immaculate Heart of Mary and the letter 'M' intertwined with the Cross signifying that Mother and Son cannot be separated. Surrounding these, binding these visual messages together, are the twelve stars of chapter twelve in the Book of Apocalypse.

The message of the Miraculous Medal is not really one of words, as few words were said during the apparitions. What is key to the apparition is the imagery announcing the Apocalypse. The hour of the "Woman clothed with the sun" is now. The second reason the imagery is remarkable is because it is essentially the same as that which is found on Juan Diego's tilma.

The Dogma of the Immaculate Conception was decreed by Blessed Pope Pius IX in 1854. Twenty-four years earlier, in 1830, the medal requested by the Virgin was to be called 'The Medal of the Immaculate Conception'. It came to be known as 'the Miraculous Medal' due to the many graces received by its wearers.

\*\*\*

13

Sister Catherine had been sleeping for only two hours when a bright light suddenly filled her room. Accompanying the light was a voice calling "Sister Laboure! Sister Laboure!" She drew open her curtain and there before her was a child wearing a long white gown. He was carrying a candle. "Come to the chapel", he said. "The Blessed Virgin awaits you. Do not be uneasy. Come. I am waiting for you."

The two of them left the dormitory and made their way to the chapel. The heavy wooden door was shut but when touched by the visitor it opened effortlessly. After entering the chapel, Sister Catherine was struck by a light so bright that her eyes could barely take it in. As she heard a voice say, "Here is the Blessed Virgin", Sister Catherine watched Our Lady move down the steps of the altar to the priest's chair where she then sat down. Any remaining hesitations vanished for Catherine as she put her hands onto the lap of her Mother.

The Virgin spoke saying, "The times are very evil. Sorrows will come upon France. The throne will be overturned. The whole world will be upset with miseries of every kind. Come to the foot of the altar. There, graces will be shed upon all who ask for them."

*The Miraculous Medal with its apocalyptic imagery and the intertwined Hearts of Jesus and Mary.*

Three months later, on the 27th of November, Catherine experienced her second apparition when the sisters were together in community prayer.

The Blessed Virgin appeared carrying a golden ball in her hand and looked toward Heaven as though offering the ball to God. Catherine heard a voice say, "The ball you see represents the whole world, especially France, and each person in particular." Sister Catherine could see different rings on the fingers of the Virgin and on each of the rings was a gem. Most of the gems were giving off bright rays of light. She was told, "These rays symbolize the graces I shed upon those who ask for them. The gems from which the rays do not fall are the graces for which souls forget to ask."

The golden ball vanished and an oval frame surrounding the Virgin then appeared. In the frame, written in gold, could be seen the words, "O, Mary, conceived without sin, pray for us who have recourse to thee." This time the Virgin told Catherine, "Have a medal struck after this model. All who wear it will receive signal graces. They should wear it around their neck. Graces will abound for persons who wear it with confidence."

The oval began turning slowly. Watching this, Sister Catherine could see two symbols overlapping each other. First there was a cross. Second, at its base was the letter 'M', representing Mary. To the bottom left was the Sacred Heart of Jesus while to the bottom right the Sorrowful Heart of Mary. Framing these were the twelve stars of the Apocalypse. Catherine went to her confessor, Father Aladel, charged with a mission. That mission was to have the medal cast. Father Aladel, known to be stubborn, was not impressed. Sister Catherine told him that she wished to remain anonymous but the medal still had to be made. Father Aladel politely agreed then went to visit his Archbishop.

The Archbishop, seeing nothing contrary to the faith, ordered the medal to be cast. An official canonical inquiry was then started which concluded by stating, "The medal is of supernatural origin. The wonders worked through it are genuine."

The Miraculous Medal, with its imagery announcing the Apocalypse, was soon being produced and reports of signal graces began pouring in. Probably the most famous of these is the conversion of Alphonse Ratisbonne, a Jewish man from a banking family in Strasbourg.

\*\*\*

After seeing his brother be exiled from the family for converting to Catholicism, Alphonse decided to put aside anything having to do with religion. A friend asked him to wear the Medal but Alphonse said he wanted nothing to do with such a silly superstition. After much badgering however, he finally consented, deciding perhaps that he would at least gain a little humor from it. His life would not be the same again.

On a trip to Rome he decided to visit the Church of Sant'Adrea della Fratte. But once inside he experienced a vision similar to what Saint Catherine had seen. He fell to his knees and in an instant was converted. He later described the event saying, "I understood all."

If the story had ended there it would be incredible enough but

Alphonse's journey was just beginning. Alphonse converted to Roman Catholicism and cut off his marriage engagement. To say it caused an uproar would not do the story justice. Within a year he was baptized and in that same year he entered the Society of Jesus. Incredibly, in 1848, he was ordained as a Jesuit priest.

With official authorization, Father Ratisbonne later left the Order and in Paris joined his brother, also a priest. They labored together for the conversion of their fellow Jews. In 1884, Father Ratisbonne passed to his eternal reward after laboring under the guidance of the Virgin for nearly twenty-six years. Today he lies buried in Jerusalem on the grounds of one of the monasteries he established.

On December 31, 1876, Sister Catherine Laboure died and in 1947, Pope Pius XII declared her to be a saint. Like Mother Mariana, Saint Catherine Laboure now lies incorrupt. Her body can be viewed at the rue de Bac.

*After wearing the Miraculous Medal, Alphonse Ratisbonne converted from Judaism and became a Jesuit priest.*

*Saint Catherine Laboure received the vision of the Miraculous Medal and now lies incorrupt.*

The Virgin of the Apocalypse had again thwarted the arrogant and the proud through the use of her little ones, and Catherine Laboure, a young French girl from a small village, had assumed her place among the holiest that the Church recognizes.

"Rome will lose the faith and become the seat of Antichrist"
The Blessed Virgin to Melanie and Maximin

# The Virgin Weeps and Announces Antichrist
## Chapter 5

<u>Our Lady of La Salette</u>
<u>1846 – La Salette, France</u>
<u>Visionaries - Melanie Calvat and Maximin Girard</u>
<u>Main Points to Consider:</u>
- The End Times Are Announced
- The Pope is Martyred
- The Promise of World Peace
- Rome Loses the Faith and Becomes the Seat of Antichrist

When the term 'Antichrist' is used it can imply several different things. First, it means anyone standing in opposition to the reign of Jesus Christ. More importantly, it means an individual who will arrive at the end of history. At La Salette both the 'end times' and the 'Antichrist' are announced by the Virgin of the Apocalypse.

\*\*\*

The village of La Salette is a remote mountain hamlet perched at the top of snow-capped peaks in south-eastern France. One day, Melanie Calvat and Maximin Girard, two illiterate shepherd children, saw a woman sitting on a rock with her face in her hands. She was wearing a crown and long flowing robes. She was also crying. She told the children to deliver a message to "all her people" and warned of immense chastisements if people failed to heed the message and respond. If people did convert however, Divine Mercy was instead offered.

The children wrote down the secret they were given, of which there were many stanzas. The prophecies concerned France and the world and many came true within a short time thereby bolstering belief in the events. The secret, among other things, announced the unleashing of Hell, apostasy in the Catholic Church, the arrival of the Antichrist and the end of history. Here we examine some of the stanzas.

7. The Society of men is on the eve of the most terrible scourges and of gravest events. Mankind must expect to be ruled with an iron rod and to drink the chalice of the wrath of God.

11. In the year 1864, Lucifer together with a large number of demons will be unloosed from Hell; they will put an end to faith little by little, even in those dedicated to God. ...several religious institutions will lose all faith and will lose many souls.

16. The holy Father will suffer a great deal. I will be with him until the end to receive his sacrifice.

21. Jesus Christ... will command His angels to have all His enemies put to death. ...Then peace will be made and man will be reconciled with God...

22. This peace among men will be short-lived.Twenty-five years of plentiful harvests will make them forget that the sins of men are the cause of all the troubles on this earth.

27. Rome will lose the faith and become the seat of the Antichrist.

33. The fire of Heaven will fall... ...Only faith will survive.

34. The abyss is opening. Here is the King of Kings of darkness. ...He will be smothered by the breath of the Archangel Saint Michael. And he will have plunged for eternity with all his followers into the everlasting chasms of hell.[1]

Like the images of Guadalupe and the Miraculous Medal, the words of La Salette are apocalyptic. According to this Church-approved apparition, Hell was unleashed in 1864 and this is the prelude to an apostasy that will engulf the Church. At Quito, the Virgin warns of Freemasonry infecting the Church which is to lead to the falling away of many religious souls. In 1984, Cardinal Ratzinger said the 'Third Secret of Fatima' dealt with "the absolute importance of history"[2] Thus, from what we have seen so far, these fully approved apparitions announce:

1) a Great Apostasy
2) the arrival of Antichrist
3) that fire will fall from the sky
4) that Hell has been unleashed upon the Earth

---

1. *Secrets of La Salette,* (Asbury, New Jersey: The 101 Foundation, 1994) pp. 11-18.
2. *Jesus* magazine, November 11, 1984, p. 79.

5) that the Catholic Church will suffer from a Masonic and secular spirit
6) that the Church will suffer a massive shortage of vocations
7) that the Virgin will crush the head of the serpent and
8) that there is to be an era of peace.

What the faithful look forward to then, is the "restoration" promised by the Virgin at Quito and the promise of peace foretold at La Salette.

*The shepherd children of La Salette, Melanie Calvat and Maximin Girard.*

*The Virgin weeps for her children and announces the coming of Antichrist.*

19

"The Immaculate Conception will be proclaimed during a time
when the Church will be strongly attacked."
Our Lord to Mother Mariana

# Purifying Water
## Chapter 6

Our Lady of the Immaculate Conception
1858 – Lourdes, France
Visionary - Saint Bernadette
Main Points to Consider:
    – Cleansing Waters Before the Fire of Fatima
    – The Triumph of the Blessed Virgin

      One series of apparitions very familiar to Catholics are those of Our Lady of Lourdes in 1858. In 1854 however, just four years previously, Blessed Pope Pius IX decreed that the Immaculate Conception was to be believed by all Catholics. This reaffirmed the vision to Saint Catherine Laboure nearly thirty years earlier when the Blessed Virgin asked to have the 'Medal of the Immaculate Conception' cast.

***

      The grotto at Massabielle, near the mountain town of Lourdes, was often called a garbage dump as that is how it was used. It was in the dank filth of the grotto that, from February 11, 1858 to July 16<sup>th</sup>, 1858, on eighteen separate occasions, the Immaculate Conception appeared to Bernarde Marie Soubirous. The girl was the oldest of five children, was small in stature (thus the nickname 'Bernadette') and of a family suffering from dire poverty.
      The visions began when Bernadette saw a Lady glide through the air and across the grotto before coming to stop on a rose bush. The Virgin did not come to speak of dreadful chastisements as she had in previous apparitions, however. Instead, at Lourdes she offered something very different: abundant and purifying water.
      Water is significant because it is the symbol of the inward grace

received at Baptism. Regarding the Sacrament, we read from Pope Eugene IV in his 'Decree for the Armenians', that,

> Holy baptism holds the first place among all the sacraments because it is the gate of spiritual life, for by it we are made members of Christ and of the body of the Church. Since through the first man death entered into the world [cf. Rom 5:12], unless we are born again of water, and of the spirit, we cannot, so saith Truth, enter into the kingdom of heaven [cf. John 3:5].

The decree continues,

> The efficacy of this sacrament is the remission of all sin, original sin and actual, and of all penalties incurred through this guilt. ...if they die before they commit any sin, they shall straightway attain the kingdom of heaven and the sight of God.[1]

It is fitting then, that she who is without sin would offer the cleansing water to her children tainted by such a defect.

On Thursday, February the 25th, the day of the ninth apparition, Bernadette was told to "wash in the fountain" but no fountain was known to exist. Bernadette says how she found it,

> The Lady said to me in a serious but friendly voice - "Go, drink and wash in the fountain". As I did not know where this fountain was, and as I did not think the matter important, I went towards the Gave *(i.e. the river next to the grotto – author)*. The Lady called me back and signed to me with Her finger to go under the Grotto to the left;  I obeyed but I did not see any water. Not knowing where to get it from, I scratched the earth and the water came. I let it get a little clear of the mud then I drank and washed.[2]

Not until the 25th of March however, did Bernadette learn the woman's name.

---

1. Council of Florence, (Basel-Ferrara-Florence), 1431-1445 A.D. Part nine., n.d., (accessed April 2, 2012) see also http://www.etwn.com/library/councils/florence.html#3., n.d., (accessed April 2, 2012)

2. Ninth Apparition - Thursday 25, February 1858, Discovery of the Miraculous Spring http://webspace.webring.com/people/bd/dave_alberts_toc/BernadetteApparitions5.html., n.d., (accessed April 2, 2012).

The Lady was standing above the rose bush, in a position very similar to that shown on the Miraculous Medal. Then slowly... she said to me in a voice vibrating with emotion, "I AM THE IMMACULATE CONCEPTION".[3]

Recalling how he felt upon hearing those words, Father Peyremale, the parish priest whose skepticism had given much grief to Bernadette, said, "I was so amazed by it that I felt myself stagger and I was on the verge of falling."[4] His reason for staggering is understandable. Only four years earlier had the Dogma become official teaching. The fourteen year old, and unlearned, Bernadette was unable to grasp the theological ramifications and would have no way of fabricating such a story. It was the proof Father Peyremale had been looking for. From that moment he fully supported the cult of Lourdes.

The symbol of water is found throughout the Old Testament. The world was first cleansed at the deluge then saved by Noah's obedience in building the Ark. Moses received water from the Rock (a prefiguring of Christ), and the Israelites were saved by the waters of the Red Sea. Tradition tells us that as the world was made clean by water, it will be consumed by fire. Fire and water figure prominently in these apparitions.

Water at Lourdes is symbolic of God's sanctifying grace. It is infinite but it also requires participation for the graces to be realized. The Virgin at Lourdes is offering her children a final chance before the fire of Fatima.

Bernadette made her First Holy Communion on Thursday, June 3rd, 1858. It was the Feast of the Blessed Sacrament. Mademoiselle Estrade, a resident of Lourdes asked, "What made you happier, Bernadette, First Holy Communion or the Apparitions?" She replied, "The two go together. They cannot be compared. I only know I was very happy on both occasions."[5] It was a simple reiteration of the Miraculous Medal. The Mother and the Cross of her Son are intertwined and cannot be separated. They work together and only serve to complement each other.

The earthly remains of Saint Bernadette, like those of Saint

---

3. Sixteenth Apparition - Thursday 25, March 1858,
http://webspace.webring.com/people/bd/dave_alberts_toc/BernadetteApparitions 11.html., n.d., (accessed April 2, 2012).
4. Ibid., Sixteenth Apparition – Thursday 25, March 1858
5. My Name is Bernadette,
http://www.ewtn.com/library/mary/bernlife.html.,n.d., (accessed April 2, 2012)

Catherine Laboure and Mother Mariana, are to this day incorrupt.

*Saint Bernadette, the visionary of Lourdes.*

"So numerous are the souls which the justice of God condemns for sins
committed against Me, that I come to ask for reparation."
Our Lady at Fatima

# Saint Michael, the Virgin and the Fires of Hell
## Chapter 7

Saint Michael the Archangel and Our Lady of the Rosary
1916-1917 – Fatima, Portugal
Visionaries: Lucia dos Santos, Francisco and Jacinta Marto
Main Points to Consider:
  - Saint Michael and the Virgin War Against Satan
  - Vision of Hell, Grave Trials for the Church
  - The Triumph of the Blessed Virgin
  - The Promise of World Peace

The apparitions at Fatima are unique. On three separate occasions
during 1916 the "Angel of Peace" appeared to three shepherd children. He
announced that men must amend their lives and sin no more and
administered the Eucharist to the children saying, "Take and drink the Body
and the Blood of Jesus Christ, horribly outraged by ungrateful men. Make
reparation for their crimes and console your God." These three visits by
Saint Michael the Archangel were the forerunner to six others from the
Blessed Virgin Mary.

We know that in the final, titanic battle between Good and Evil, Saint
Michael the Archangel and the Blessed Virgin Mary will war against Satan
and his followers. Fatima is a prefiguring of this struggle.

\*\*\*

On the thirteenth of the month, from May until October,1917, Jacinta
and Francisco Marto and Lucia dos Santos, cousins, reported seeing a 'Lady
of light'. The Lady told the children she came "from Heaven". The Virgin,
who appeared no older than sixteen herself, asked if they would return to the
same location at the same time for six months. She also asked if they would
be willing to make sacrifices to save the souls of sinners. Like Mother
Mariana at Quito, they agreed and were told, "Then you will have much to

suffer but the grace of God will be your comfort." From that moment forward they performed heroic sacrifices which included drinking no water in the scorching summer heat and wearing a rough cord of rope around their waists, a penance that caused them to bleed frequently.

On her third visit, the Virgin opened her hands at shoulder height. Light proceeded from them and penetrated the earth and the children were shown a vision of Hell. In her memoirs, Sister Lucia described the vision in detail:

> Our Lady showed us a great sea of fire which seemed to be under the earth. Plunged in this fire were demons and souls in human form, like transparent burning embers, all blackened or burnished bronze, floating about in the conflagration, now raised into the air by the flames that issued from within themselves together with great clouds of smoke, now falling back on every side like sparks in a huge fire, without weight or equilibrium, and amid shrieks and groans of pain and despair, which horrified us and made us tremble with fear. The demons could be distinguished by their terrifying and repulsive likeness to frightful and unknown animals, all black and transparent. This vision lasted but an instant. How can we ever be grateful enough to our kind heavenly Mother, who had already prepared us by promising, in the first apparition, to take us to heaven. Otherwise, I think we would have died of fear and terror.[1]

The Virgin explained the vision saying, "You have seen Hell where the souls of poor sinners go. To save them God wishes to establish in the world the devotion to my Immaculate Heart. If people will do what I shall tell you, many souls will be saved..." On another occasion she told the children, "Pray, pray very much and make sacrifices for sinners, for many souls go to Hell because they have no one to make sacrifices and to pray for them." The Virgin then asked that a prayer be added at the end of each decade of the Rosary: "O my Jesus, forgive us our sins. Save us from the fires of Hell. Lead all souls to Heaven, especially those who are most in need."

---

1. Christopher A. Ferrara, *The Secret Still Hidden,* pp. 9 – 10. Also, Congregation for the Doctrine of the Faith, *The Message of Fatima* (Vatican City: Libreria Editrice Vaticana, 2000) (*Message*), p. 13.

The children suffered ridicule from hardened skeptics and bewildered family members. Lucia, being the oldest, became the groups' spokesman. Pleading, she asked the Virgin to perform a miracle to show they were telling the truth. Incredibly, providing both the time and location beforehand, the Virgin responded, "I will perform a miracle so that all may believe". The promise of a miracle spread like wildfire and on October 13th everyone was there to see it.

It had started raining the night before and continued unabated throughout the night. By the late morning, the Cova de Iria, site of the apparitions, had been turned into a vast sea of mud. But the people would not be deterred. They continued to come, wave after wave after wave. The wealthy drove the latest automobile while the others made the necessary trek on foot from wherever they lived. This gathering of humanity was comprised of the devout, the curious and the vehemently opposed. The press, religious and secular, came out in numbers. This group, estimated to be 70,000 strong, withstood the heavy rain waiting to observe Heaven's great miracle.

*70,000 waiting for a miracle at the Cova de Iria.*

As the last apparition drew to a close the Virgin spoke her final words to the children, "People must not offend Our Lord anymore, for He is already greatly offended." Turning to go, she pointed to the sun. The long-awaited miracle began.

Immediately, the heavy rain clouds were torn asunder. Only the sun was left shining in a now clear sky. It took on a dull, opaque 'silverish' color and could be viewed easily with the naked eye. The 'silverish' sun then began shooting out fantastic bursts of light in all colors of the rainbow. The colors from the previously dull disk were now changing the hue of the surrounding area. When radiating blue, the ground, trees and clothing of everyone present was also blue. When it was red, likewise red. After a few minutes the sun stopped but just as suddenly began revolving again, repeating feverishly the first display. It stopped again before beginning yet a third and final time. But this time the sun began *falling* on the now terrified crowd. Those who moments before were standing spellbound, now stood crying out loud. Terrified, many started begging forgiveness while others confessed their sins in public. Doctor Almeida Garrett described the experience saying,

> We suddenly heard a clamor, like a cry of anguish of that entire crowd. The sun, in fact, keeping its rapid movement of rotation, seemed to free itself from the firmament and blood-red, to plunge towards the earth, threatening to crush us with its fiery mass. Those were some terrifying seconds.[2]

After a display that caused hardened sinners to weep and confess their sins in public, the sun returned to its regular position and shone with its normal intensity. It was no longer possible to look directly at it and everyone found their clothing was dry due to the intensity of heat. Ten minutes before the 70,000 onlookers stood wallowing in a sea of mud. Now, a dumbstruck crowd walked away under the afternoon sun. The promised miracle had occurred and it was terrifying. It had been performed by the Virgin of the Apocalypse.

*"I will perform a miracle so that all may believe."*

*Witnessing the beautiful then terrifying spectacle.*

So that "all may believe", the time and location of the miracle had been announced months in advance. The anti-clerical press had gone to ridicule the children, their dim-witted friends and religion in general. But to

---

2. Father Paul Kramer, *The Devil's Final Battle,* (Terryville, Conn., The Missionary Association, 2002), p. 11.

their credit they printed their experiences and the newspapers ran their articles accompanied by photographs of the event. Friend and foe alike were believers that day and they agreed on one thing: the powers of Heaven were indeed shaken. The sun had danced ominously in the sky.

At Fatima, the Blessed Virgin asked the faithful to do two things. First, she asked them to recite a third of the Rosary everyday ("o terço") in order to bring peace to the world and an end to the war (World War I was then raging). Second, she asked that Devotion to the Immaculate Heart be established and granted this alongside it: "To those who embrace it, I promise salvation. These souls will be loved by God like flowers placed by me to adorn His throne."[3]

As noted, these apparitions are steeped in images of the apocalypse but Fatima is still unique for several reasons. First, the magnitude of the event is without equal in the history of the Church. It was promised, it occurred, and it was terrifying. Second, the time and location were announced beforehand. Anyone wishing to see the miracle only had to be present.

Fatima is today, as it was then, a cry from Heaven. At Quito the Virgin announced "the arrival of my hour" and a "complete restoration". Visiting Sister Lucia in her convent in Tuy, Spain, in 1929, the Blessed Virgin gave the exact formula on how this peace would come about. There she announced,

> The moment has come in which God asks of the Holy Father to make, and to order that in union with him, and at the same time, all the bishops of the world make the Consecration of Russia to My Immaculate Heart promising to convert it because of this day of prayer and worldwide reparation.[4]

To clarify this, Sister Lucia stated later, "Our Lady commanded that the Holy Father consecrate Russia to Her Immaculate Heart and that he command all the bishops to do it also in union with him at the same time."[5]

The debate rages still but it seems the consecrations of Pope John Paul II failed to fulfill Heaven's mandate on three accounts. First, on neither

---

3. Joseph A. Pelletier, A. A., *The Sun Danced at Fatima* (New York, NY: Doubleday, 1983), p. 48.

4. Mark Fellows, *Sister Lucia – Apostle of Mary's Immaculate Heart,* (Buffalo, NY: Immaculate Heart Publications, 2007), p. 121.

5. Ibid., p. 150.

occasion did the Holy Father consecrate Russia, and Russia alone, to the Immaculate Heart of Mary. This can be read in his addresses. Second, the Holy Father did not order every bishop to take part in the event which is an integral aspect of the consecration. Sister Lucia spoke specifically of this on two occasions. Third, the promised result of the consecration is that the world will be "given a period of peace". This is also the prophecy of Quito and La Salette. Simply put then, it seems the result of John Paul II's consecrations runs contrary to the prophecies of these fully approved apparitions which fortell the triumph of the Immaculate Heart.

In 2000, the Vatican announced that it would release, finally, the 'Third Secret of Fatima'. According to the Congregation for the Doctrine of the Faith, here is the vision seen by the children without the accompanying words given by the Virgin to explain it, which she always did.

> … At the left of Our Lady and a little above, we saw an Angel with flaming sword in his left hand; flashing, it gave out flames that looked as though they would set the world on fire; but they died out in contact with the splendor that Our Lady radiated towards him from her right hand, pointing to the earth with his right hand, the Angel cried out in a loud voice: 'Penance, Penance, Penance!'. And we saw in an immense light that is God: 'something similar to how people appear in a mirror when they pass in front of it' a Bishop dressed in White 'we had the impression that it was the Holy Father'. Other Bishops, Priests, men and women religious going up a steep mountain, at the top of which there was a big Cross of rough-hewn trunks as of a cork-tree with the bark; before reaching there the Holy Father passed through a big city half in ruins and half trembling with halting step, afflicted with pain and sorrow, he prayed for the souls of the corpses he met on his way; having reached the top of the mountain, on his knees at the foot of the big Cross he was killed by a group of soldiers who fired bullets and arrows at him, and in the same way there died one after another the other Bishops, Priests, men and women Religious, and various lay people of different ranks and positions. Beneath the two arms of the Cross there were two Angels each with a crystal aspersorium in his hand, in which they gathered up the blood of the Martyrs and with it sprinkled the souls that were making their way to God.[6]

---

6. Ibid., pp. 188-189.

Just as the Miracle of the Sun was harrowing, so too was the seers' vision. Foretold is the liquidation of Catholic faithful, bishops, clergy and even the pope. The liquidation is so great in fact, that it requires four angels to collect the blood of those already killed and sprinkle it on the others about to be. This approved vision prophesies the murder of a pope but it had been prophesied earlier at La Salette. There the Virgin had announced, "The Holy Father will suffer much. I will be with him until the end to receive his sacrifice."

In addition to seeing the apparitions as a group, each of the children also had mystical experiences of their own. Francisco for instance, was confronted by "one of those big beasts that we saw in Hell." And Jacinta experienced disturbing prophecies regarding the Pope and the Church. In her memoirs Sister Lucia related how Jacinta called out to her,

> "Didn't you see the Holy Father? ...I don't know how it was, but I saw the Holy Father in a very large house. He was kneeling by a table with his face in his hands and he was crying. Outside the house were many people. Some of them were throwing stones at him, others were cursing him and saying many ugly words at him. Poor Holy Father, we must pray for him a great deal.[7]

In 1957, Sister Lucia gave an approved interview to Father Fuentes who was then acting officially as the postulator for the beatifications of Jacinta and Francisco. After publicizing the interview however, Father Fuentes was removed from his position. Thereafter, Sister Lucia was silenced by the Vatican and forbidden to say anything more regarding the apparitions. This edict remained in force until her death. Father Fuentes was replaced by Father Joaquin Alonso who reached the conclusion that what was said in the interview was nothing more than what Sister Lucia had stated continuously in her writings. Among other things, Sister Lucia had communicated the following to Father Fuentes,

> That which afflicts the Immaculate Heart of Mary and the Heart of Jesus is the fall of religious and priestly souls. The devil knows that religious and priests who fall away from their beautiful vocation drag numerous souls to hell. ...The devil wishes to take possession of consecrated souls. He tries to corrupt them in order to lull to sleep

---

7. *The Sun Danced at Fatima,* p. 66.

the souls of laypeople and thereby lead them to final impenitence.[8]

The prophecy of Quito had come to pass. In the wake of Vatican II, when an estimated 35,000 Catholic priests alone, not including brothers and nuns, deserted their vocations after being laicized by Pope Paul VI, it would be tough to argue that the devil did not succeed in exactly what the Blessed Virgin was warning against. The 'secular spirit of Freemasonry', foretold at Quito, and the apostasy foretold at La Salette, had indeed infected the Church. The "auto-demolition" lamented by Pope Paul VI was very much suffocating the Catholic world.

In 1917, Lucia dos Santos was told she would not be going to Heaven with Jacinta and Francisco. Instead, Sister Lucia would "remain some time longer" in order to propagate the devotion of reparation on the First Five Saturday's to the Immaculate Heart of Mary. In 2005, at the age of ninety-seven, she passed to her eternal reward.

---

8. *Sister Lucia – Apostle of Mary's Immaculate Heart,* p. 265.

"We must disagree with these prophets of doom, who are always forecasting worse disasters, as though the end of the world were at hand."
Pope John XXIII

"In order that the world might know his anger, the Heavenly Father is preparing to inflict a great chastisement on all mankind. ...Fire will fall from the sky and wipe out a great part of humanity."
The Blessed Virgin to Sister Agnes

# Fire Falls From the Sky
## Chapter 8

Our Lady of Akita
1973 - Akita, Japan
Visionary - Sister Agnes Katsuko Sasagawa
Main Points to Consider:
  - A Wooden Statue Weeps, Sweats and Receives the Stigmata
  - Fire Will Fall From the Sky
  - A Large Portion of Mankind is Wiped Out

When Sister Agnes Sasagawa heard the voice of the Blessed Virgin in 1973, she belonged to the contemplative Order 'Handmaids of the Sacred Heart of Jesus in the Holy Eucharist.' She was also deaf. Miraculously, Sister Agnes later regained her hearing and in the course of her experiences with the supernatural also received the stigmata in her left hand. Finally, she would be given a message that announced "fire will fall from the sky and wipe out a great part of humanity."

After investigating the events for eight years, local bishop John Ito released this statement on April 22, 1984, "I authorize that all of the diocese entrusted to me venerate the Holy Mother of Akita."[1]

\*\*\*

While at prayer, Sister Agnes witnessed rays of light coming from

1. Akita, Japan (1973 – 81), n.d., http://www.miraclehunter.com/marian_apparitions/akita/index.html., (accessed March 28, 2012).

inside the tabernacle. It was June 12, 1973. She witnessed the same light again on the two days following but as unexpectedly as they had come the lights then ceased. Almost two weeks later, on June 28, the stigmata appeared in the palm of Sister Agnes's left hand. The stigmata was in the shape of a cross, produced copious quantities of blood and was excruciatingly painful.

Then on July 6th, the convent's wooden statue of the Virgin also developed the stigmata, this time on the right hand. The drops of blood were seen by the sisters and this was repeated on four different occasions. The stigmata would remain until the 29th of September.

When the stigmata disappeared the statue began to sweat, especially on the forehead and neck. Finally, on January 4, 1975, the statue began to weep and continued to do so over a period of more than six and one half years. The weeping was photographed and recorded by a Japanese film crew and documented on 101 different occasions. Not until 1982 did the weeping finally cease.

*The wooden statue of Akita. It sweat on the neck and forehead, developed the stigmata on the hand and wept on 101 different occasions.*

*Sister Agnes Sasagawa of Akita. The stigmatist was miraculously cured of her deafness and saw her guardian angel four different times.*

The first message of the Virgin stated,

Pray in reparation for the sins of men... Most Sacred Heart of Jesus, truly present in the Holy Eucharist, I consecrate my body and soul to be entirely one with Your Heart, being sacrificed at every instant on all the altars of the world and giving praise to the Father pleading for the coming of His Kingdom.

When the prayer was finished, the Blessed Virgin said, "Pray very much for the Pope, Bishops, and Priests... Continue to pray very much... very much."[2]

The second message occurred on August 3, 1973.

In order that the world might know His anger, the Heavenly Father is preparing to inflict a great chastisement on all mankind. With my Son I have intervened so many times to appease the wrath of the Father. I have prevented the coming of calamities by offering Him the sufferings of the Son on the Cross, His Precious Blood, and beloved souls who console Him forming a cohort of victim souls. Prayer, penance and courageous sacrifices can soften the Father's anger. I desire this also from your community, that it love poverty, that it sanctify itself and pray in reparation for the ingratitude and outrages of so many men...[3]

On October 13th, the anniversary of the Miracle of the Sun, Sister Agnes received her final message. It is a hair-raising continuation of Quito, La Salette and Fatima. Like Quito and La Salette, it announces "fire will fall from the sky". It also announces that a large portion of mankind will be completely wiped out and speaks of the chastisements to be suffered by the Church in the days ahead.

As I told you, if men do not repent and better themselves, the Father will inflict a terrible punishment on all humanity. It will be a punishment greater than the deluge, such as one will never have seen before. Fire will fall from the sky and will wipe out a great part of humanity, the good as well as the bad, sparing neither priests nor faithful. The survivors will find themselves so desolate that they will envy the dead. The only arms which will remain for you will be the

2. Father Teiji Yasuda, O.S.V., *Akita – The Tears and Message of Our Lady* (Asbury, New Jersey: 101 Foundation Inc., 1989), pp. 35-36.
3. Ibid., p. 62.

Rosary and the Sign left by My Son. Each day recite the prayers of the Rosary. With the Rosary, pray for the Pope, the bishops and priests.

The work of the devil will infiltrate even into the Church in such a way that one will see cardinals opposing cardinals, bishops against other bishops. The priests who venerate me will be scorned and opposed by their confreres... churches and altars sacked; the Church will be full of those who accept compromises and the demon will press many priests and consecrated souls to leave the service of the Lord.

The demon will be especially implacable against souls consecrated to God. The thought of the loss of so many souls is the cause of my sadness. If sins increase in number and gravity, there will be no longer pardon for them. ...Pray very much the prayers of the Rosary. I alone am able still to save you from the calamities which approach. Those who place their confidence in me will be saved.[4]

In 1988, the former Philippine ambassador to the Vatican, Howard Dee, told *Inside the Vatican* that, "Cardinal Ratzinger personally confirmed to me that these two messages, of Fatima and Akita, are essentially the same."[5] At Fatima, the Virgin told the children, "Continue to say the beads everyday in honor of Our Lady of the Rosary to obtain peace for the world... for she alone can succor you."[6] At Akita, likewise.

The almost total collapse of the religious life has led to the kind of squalor that the Church is now being subjected to on a regular basis and the parade of horrors continues unabated while "the voices of those who should speak remain silent." The "auto-demolition" rolls on while the Church continues with its sufferings, afflicted by pitiful Mass attendance, homosexual scandals within the clergy, Barney Blessings, abysmal catechesis and bishops who openly proclaim ideas contrary to the Church they represent without suffering the least reprimand.

Especially perplexing is the sad fact that many of the faithful and priests who simply want to retain an element of sanity are treated with

---

4. Ibid., pp. 77-78.

5. *Catholic World News,* October 11, 2001

6. Joseph A. Pelletier, A.A., *The Sun Danced at Fatima,* (New York, NY: An Image Book, 1983), p. 59.

contempt by their local bishops.  This is not news of course, it is simply the state of the modern Catholic Church.

# Part Two

"The Blessed Virgin was warning us against apostasy in the Church."
Cardinal Oddi on the '3ʳᵈ Secret of Fatima'

# What Secret?
## Chapter 9

The Pope of 1960, Pope John XXIII, was supposed to release the 'Third Secret' of Fatima. But as 1960 came and went, the Catholic world could only stand along the sidelines and watch. Everyone waited with bated breath. And they continued to wait. When asked why he had chosen not to release it, Pope John XXIII said, "It does not concern my pontificate." Clearly then, it would concern someone's. Of course, the real news of the day was the convening of the Second Vatican Council which would be coming up shortly in 1962. Nearly thirty years earlier, however, Monsignor Pacelli, the future Pope Pius XII, was already grieving over what lay in store for the Church in the days ahead. In 1931 he stated,

> I am worried by the Blessed Virgin's messages to Lucia of Fatima. This persistence of Mary about the dangers which menace the Church is a divine warning against the suicide of altering the Faith, in Her liturgy, Her theology, and Her soul. ...I hear all around me innovators who wish to dismantle the Sacred Chapel, destroy the universal flame of the Church, reject Her ornaments and make Her feel remorse for Her historical past.[1]

It is a well known fact that the innovators Pacelli was grieving over had already been stirring in the ranks of the hierarchy for some time. Many of these liberal theologians, officially condemned by Rome, then became the experts (peritii) at the Second Vatican Council. Father Wiltgen, in his book *The Rhine Flows Into the Tiber,* chronicled these events as they happened. He summarized that liberal theologians and their cliques misappropriated the schema for the Council then assumed majority positions in the decision making process. Pius XII, as Pope, decided against calling a Council for this

---

1. Christopher A. Ferrara, *The Secret Still Hidden,* (Pound Ridge, New York: Good Counsel Publications, 2008), p. 31. Also, Msgr. Georges Roche, *Pie XII Devant L'Histoire* (Paris: Editions Robert Laffont, 1972), p. 52.

very reason. He knew that Modernism, "the synthesis of all heresies" so famously crushed by Pope Saint Pius X, had been seeping through the cracks for years. But it had already been foretold by the Blessed Virgin. At Quito she had announced that the Church would take on the spirit of Freemasonry and this spirit would lead to a massive shortage in vocations.

*Pope Pius XII grieved over the prophetic words of Fatima and decided against calling an ecumenical council.*

Pope Pius XII knew that many of the proponents of the 'New Theology' then festering were becoming, or had already become, famous. In their ranks were the likes of Teilhard de Chardin, Karl Rahner, Hans Kung, and a great many others. After Pius's death, Pope John XXIII would famously "throw open the windows of the Church". Based on the exodus of clergy after this happened though, it would be hard not to conclude that what blew in was the spirit of the world and Freemasonry foretold by the Virgin at Quito.

That Vatican II altered substantially the face of the Roman Catholic Church is something everyone could agree on. Might one summarize then, that when Pope Paul VI placed Archbishop Annabale Bugnini, strongly suspected of being a Freemason, in charge of the liturgical reform and brought in six Protestant ministers to help create the Novus Ordo Missae, he set in motion a break with Tradition the likes of which had not been seen before in the history of the Church? No pope had ever brought in anyone clinging to a heretical position to create, or help create, the Church's official liturgy. It would seem that the liberalism unleashed upon the Church at Vatican II represents that which Pacelli had grieved over thirty years earlier, and that which the Blessed Virgin had warned against at Quito even earlier still.

*Pope Paul VI (on right) with the six Protestant ministers who helped create the Novus Ordo Missae.*

*Archbishop Annabale Bugnini, the man in charge of the liturgical reform.*

Several quotes from the highest ranking Church officials, including the Pope, speak of the 'Third Secret of Fatima' as something that is still playing out, not as something that is already finished. Before an audience at Fulda, Germany in 1980, John Paul II was questioned "What about the 'Third Secret of Fatima'? Should it not have already been published by 1960?" The Pope responded by saying,

> Given the seriousness of the contents, my predecessors in the Petrine office diplomatically preferred to postpone publication so as not to encourage the world power of Communism to make certain moves. On the other hand, it should be sufficient for all Christians to know this: if there is a message in which it is written that the oceans will flood whole areas of the earth, and that from one moment to the next millions of people will perish, truly the publication of such a message is no longer something to be so much desired.

> Many wish to know simply from curiosity and a taste for the sensational, but they forget that knowledge also implies

responsibility. They only seek the satisfaction of their curiosity, and that is dangerous if at the same time they are not disposed to do something, and if they are convinced that it is impossible to do anything against evil". Grabbing his rosary, he continued, "Here is the remedy against this evil. Pray, pray, and ask for nothing more. Leave everything else to the Mother of God."

When asked, "What is going to happen to the Church?", the Pope offered this chilling response:

We must prepare ourselves to suffer great trials before long, such as will demand of us a disposition to give up even life, and a total dedication to Christ and for Christ. ...With your and my prayer it is possible to mitigate this tribulation, but it is no longer possible to avert it, because only thus can the Church be effectively renewed. How many times has the renewal of the Church sprung from blood! This time, too, it will not be otherwise. We must be strong and prepared, and trust in Christ and His Mother, and be very, very assiduous in praying the Rosary.[2]

This, of course, simply reaffirms the messages of Fatima, La Salette and the dream of Saint John Bosco to be examined in the next chapter: that the Pope is to be martyred along with many, many others. At Fulda, we are told that we must prepare and seemingly expect, to become martyrs ourselves.

Pope John Paul II says that entire sections of the Earth will be under water and millions of people will perish from one moment to the next. The messages of Akita and La Salette tell us that fire will fall from the sky. Either way you look at it, it makes you hope you are not around to see it. And these events of course, are in conjunction with the ominous dancing of the sun witnessed by 70,000 at Fatima.

---

2. www.fatima.org/thirdsecret/fulda.asp

*Pope John Paul II
warns of great
upheavals in the
Church and nature.*

In Cardinal Ratzinger's now famous interview with *Jesus* magazine, he was asked why the Secret was not released in 1960. The Cardinal replied,

> Because, according to the judgment of the Popes, it adds nothing (literally: 'nothing different') to what a Christian must know concerning what derives from Revelation: i.e., a radical call for conversion; the absolute importance of history; the dangers threatening the faith and the life of the Christian, and therefore of the world. And then the importance of the 'novissimi' (the last events at the end of time). If it is not made public - at least for the time being - it is in order to prevent religious prophecy from being mistaken for a quest for the sensational (literally: 'for sensationalism'). But the things contained in this 'Third Secret' correspond to what has been announced in Scripture and has been said again and again in many other Marian apparitions... Conversion and penitence are the essential conditions for 'salvation'.[3]

In that same year the bishop of Fatima, Bishop do Amaral, said the Secret concerned "our faith". He went on to add, "The loss of faith of a continent is worse than the annihilation of a nation; and it is true that faith is

---

3. *Jesus* magazine, November 11, 1984, p.79.

continually diminishing in Europe".[4]

As recently as 2010, while visiting Fatima to celebrate the 93rd anniversary of the apparitions, Pope Benedict XVI fielded questions while on the Papal plane. Making it clear that the Secret has not been fulfilled, the Holy Father said there are,

> ...future realities of the Church which are little by little developing and revealing themselves. ...Thus, it is true that beyond the moment indicated in the vision, it is spoken, it is seen, the necessity of a passion of the Church that naturally is reflected in the person of the Pope; but the Pope is in the Church, and therefore the sufferings of the Church are what is announced...[5]

When Sister Lucia was pressed for details regarding the Secret, she simply said, "It is in the Gospel and the Apocalypse. Read them!" On the anniversary of the first apparition in Fatima, before 500,000, the Pope proclaimed, "Whoever thinks that the prophetic mission of Fatima is concluded deceives himself."[6]

---

4. *The Secret Still Hidden,* p. 39.
5. Pope Benedict XVI – 2005 to present,
http://www.fatimaforbeginners.org/index.php/fatima/approvals-by-the-popes/46,
n.d., (accessed on April 3, 2012).
6. Ibid., (accessed on April 3, 2012).

Satan: "I can destroy your Church."
Christ: "Then go ahead and do so. You have the time, you have the power."
Pope Leo XIII – Locution

# The Pope, the Celestial Dance and Other Modern Phenomena
# Chapter 10

<u>1862</u>
<u>Prophetic Dream of the Two Columns</u>
<u>Saint John Bosco</u>
  - Duress in the Church
  - The Pope is Martyred
  - The Promise of Peace

Saint John Bosco received many prophetic dreams regarding the youths under his care. Not all of the dreams however, concerned his boys. One dream deals with the wounding and martyrdom of a pope before a period of peace ensues. The dream reiterates the apparitions and the promise of the Virgin.

> The vast expanse of water is covered with a formidable array of ships in battle formation... All are heavily armed with cannons, incendiary bombs, and firearms of all sorts - even books - and are heading toward one stately ship, mightier than them all. As they try to close in, they try to ram it, set it on fire, and cripple it as much as possible.

> This stately vessel is shielded by a flotilla escort... in this midst of this endless sea, two solid columns, a short distance apart, soar high into the sky: one is surmounted by a statue of the Immaculate Virgin at whose feet a large inscription reads: Help of Christians; the other far loftier and sturdier, supports a [Communion] Host of proportionate size and bears beneath it the inscription Salvation of believers.

The flagship commander - the Roman Pontiff - seeing the enemy's fury and his auxiliary ships' very grave predicament, summons his captains to a conference. However, as they discuss their strategy, a furious storm breaks out and they must return to their ships. When the storm abates, the Pope again summons his captains as the flagship keeps on its course. But the storm rages again. Standing at the helm, the Pope strains every muscle to steer his ship between the two columns from whose summits hang many anchors and strong hooks linked to chains.

The entire enemy fleet closes in to intercept and sink the flagship at all costs. They bombard it with everything they have: books and pamphlets, incendiary bombs, firearms, cannons. The battle rages ever more furious. Beaked prows ram the flagship again and again, but to no avail, as, unscathed and undaunted, it keeps on its course. At times a formidable ram splinters a gaping hole into its hull, but, immediately, a breeze from the two columns instantly seals the gash. Meanwhile, enemy cannons blow up, firearms and beaks fall to pieces, ships crack up and sink to the bottom. In blind fury the enemy takes to hand-to-hand combat, cursing and blaspheming. Suddenly the Pope falls, seriously wounded. He is instantly helped up but, struck down a second time, dies. A shout of victory rises from the enemy and wild rejoicing sweeps their ships. But no sooner is the Pope dead than another takes his place. The captains of the auxiliary ships elected him so quickly that the news of the Pope's death coincides with that of his successor's election. The enemy's self-assurance wanes.

Breaking through all resistance, the new Pope steers his ship safely between the two columns and moors it to the two columns; first to the one surmounted by the Host, and then to the other, topped by the statue of the Virgin. At this point something unexpected happens. The enemy ships panic and disperse, colliding with and scuttling each other. Some auxiliary ships which had gallantly fought alongside their flagship are the first to tie up at the two columns.

Many others, which had fearfully kept far away from the fight, stand still, cautiously waiting until the wrecked enemy ships vanish under the waves. Then, they too head for the two columns, tie up at the swinging hooks, and ride safe and tranquil beside their flagship.

A great calm now covers the sea.[1]

Saint Don Bosco explained this dream saying,

Very grave trials await the Church. What we have suffered so far is almost nothing compared to what is going to happen. The enemies of the Church are symbolized by the ships which strive their utmost to sink the flagship. Only two things can save us in such a grave hour: devotion to Mary and frequent Communion. Let us do our very best to use these two means and have others use them everywhere.[2]

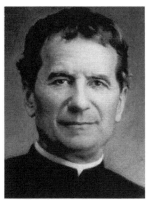

*Saint Don Bosco*
*prophetic dream warns*
*of a martyred pope and*
*grave trials awaiting*
*the Church.*

In the dream, after one pope is murdered another takes his place. That pontiff then steers the ship toward the two great Catholic beacons: the Eucharist and the Virgin Mary. Immediately thereafter, a great peace follows. Everything is calm. It was promised at Fatima that, "In the end my Immaculate Heart will triumph, the Holy Father will consecrate Russia to me and the world will be given a period of peace." At Quito the Virgin spoke of

---

1. Don Bosco's Prophecy of the Two Columns,
http://www.theotokos.org.uk/pages/fatima/donbosco.html, n.d.,
(accessed on April 3, 2012)
2. Ibid., n.d., (accessed on April 3, 2012)

"...The arrival of my hour when I... will dethrone the proud and cursed Satan... there will be occasions when all will seem to be lost and paralyzed. This, then, will be the happy beginning of the complete restoration.."[3] And finally, at La Salette the Blessed Virgin said,

> The holy Father will suffer much. I will be with him until the end to receive his sacrifice. ...Then Jesus Christ... will command to His angels that all His enemies be put to death. ...the persecutors of the Church of Jesus Christ and all men devoted to sin will perish... Then peace, the reconciliation of God with men will be made; ...charity will flower everywhere...

The dream of Saint John Bosco shows definite congruency with the messages of the Blessed Virgin and, in fact, tells an identical story. Great trials await us says Saint Don Bosco. Pope John Paul II says we can expect massive upheavals in nature, a flooded planet and "millions perishing from one moment to the next". The Blessed Virgin has warned the Church repeatedly of apostasy, the coming Antichrist, fire falling from the sky and the blood of martyred popes, bishops and faithful.

The remains of Saint Don Bosco, like Mother Mariana, Saint Catherine Laboure, Saint Bernadette and Blessed Jacinta, now lie incorrupt. His remains can be viewed at the Basilica of Mary Our Help in Turin, Italy.


October 13th, 1884
Vatican City
Locution of Pope Leo XIII
 - The Ominous Date of October the 13th
 - Satan is Allowed to Crush the Church and Seduce Many Religious Souls

On October 13th, 1884, thirty-three years to the day before the Miracle of the Sun, Pope Leo XIII had finished celebrating his daily Mass. When he stopped at the foot of the altar his face went pale and he stood motionless for several minutes. Recovering, he went to the sacristy and composed his famous Prayer to Saint Michael the Archangel. It was to be said at the end of every Low Mass, which it was until being dropped after the Second Vatican Council. This is the conversation he was permitted to hear between Christ and Satan,

---

3. *Our Lady of Good Success – Prophecies For Our Times,* p. 58, 55.

50

Satan: "I can destroy your Church."
Christ: "You can? Then go ahead and do so."
Satan: "To do so I need more time."
Christ: "How much time, how much power?"
Satan: "Seventy-five to one-hundred years, and a greater power over those who will give themselves to my service."
Christ: "You have the time, you have the power. Do with them what you will."

A period of seventy-five to one-hundred years would approximately mean the years from 1959/1960 through 1984/1985 and this is telling. It was in this period that thousands of priests and other consecrated souls began an unprecedented exodus from the Church, the likes of which had never been seen before. And it was that which Sister Lucia had warned about in her interview with Father Fuentes in 1957. To this day the Church has not recovered.

*Pope Leo XIII - his locution revealed that Satan would be allowed to crush and almost destroy the Church.*

More disturbing is that no signs of a great restoration can be seen. With her religious ranks decimated and little spiritual combat in the offing, the Church has embraced, and is being overrun by, the spirit of the world as foretold by the Blessed Virgin at Quito.

Miracle of the Sun
1950
Vatican City
Vision of Pope Pius XII
 - The Apocalyptic Dancing of the Sun
 - It is Witnessed by the Pope on Four Different Occasions

We read from Zenit.org that, according to his own account, Pope Pius XII witnessed the foreboding celestial dance on four different occasions, more than any other person in history. He stated, "I have seen the 'Miracle of the Sun' this is the pure truth." Describing the sun's movements he said, "It moved outward slightly, either spinning, or moving from left to right and vice versa. Within the sphere, you could see marked movements with total clarity and without interruption."[4]

The Pope first witnessed the event while taking a "habitual walk in the Vatican Gardens". He had just arrived at the statue of Our Lady of Lourdes and was struck by the vision "that before now I had never seen."[5] The Pope later explained that he saw the same phenomena on "the 31st of October and Nov. 1, the day of the definition of the dogma of the Assumption, and then again Nov. 8, and after that, no more."[6]

In 1952, two years later, the Virgin appeared to Sister Lucia again, this time stating sadly,

> Make it known to the Holy Father that I am always awaiting the Consecration of Russia to My Immaculate Heart. Without this consecration, Russia will not be able to convert, nor the world have peace.[7]

---

4. http://www.zenit.org.html., n.d., (accessed on March 27, 2012)
5. Ibid., n.d., (accessed on March 27, 2012)
6. Ibid., n.d., (accessed on March 27, 2012)
7. *Sister Lucia – Apostle of Mary's Immaculate Heart,* p. 157.

When announcing the signs that will signify the 'end times', in the Gospel of Luke Jesus warns "there shall be signs in the sun..." and "the powers of heaven shall be moved." (Luke 21:25-26) History has now shown us that on five separate occasions the sun has danced in the sky and the powers of Heaven have definitely moved. Something is knocking at the door.

"I will give of the fountain of the water of life."
Apocalypse 21:6

# Points to Ponder
# Chapter 11

These messages can be reduced to having three key components:

1) Turn back to God or suffer great spiritual and physical chastisements.

2) Fatima was an apocalyptic miracle given so that "all may believe". It was promised and it was terrifying. Devotion to the Immaculate Heart is now our only recourse as many souls are on the road to Hell.

3) The Pope of 1960 was supposed to release the secret of Fatima but did not. Many have read it and many references have been made to it. It is recorded in the Gospel and the Apocalypse. It speaks of "nations being wiped off the face of the earth" and "apostasy" in the Catholic Church.

Regarding the triumph of the Immaculate Heart and how it will happen is anyone's guess. All we know is that the ways of man are not the ways of God. We are reminded of the Virgin's words to Mother Mariana, "I, in a marvelous way, will dethrone the proud and cursed Satan, trampling under my feet and fettering him in the infernal abyss." The only thing we can say for sure is that however it happens, it will be unexpected.

The apparitions present us with a recurring theme: the heel of the Virgin crushes the serpent but not before massive upheavals rock a Church that has shaken off its very essence. We see that "before long", according to Pope John Paul II, large numbers of Catholics, including the Pope, may likely be liquidated. Coupled with this are titanic forces being unleashed in nature that will "wipe out a great portion of humanity." The awe-struck crowd at Fatima watched the heavens shake loose and Pius XII watched it too.

Mary asked that the Devotion to her Immaculate Heart be established promising to save the souls of sinners by this means. She also said, "Only she can save you." Jesus appeared to Sister Lucia and told her He wanted Devotion to the Immaculate Heart to be placed alongside His own, which is in conjunction with the obverse image on the Miraculous Medal seen by Saint Catherine Laboure. Following the apparitions at Lourdes, Saint Bernadette simply stated, "The two go together..."

One wonders about the scriptural passages to which Cardinal Ratzinger was referring if Akita announces "Fire will fall from the sky...", La Salette says "Rome will become the seat of the Antichrist" and Pope John Paul II warns us that, "from one moment to the next, millions of people will perish" in addition to readying ourselves to become martyrs. If the Secret can be read in the Gospel, and has been spoken of "again and again in many other Marian apparitions", then it is no secret at all. Why then, did the Vatican not simply release it in 1960 as was supposed to be done?

Tradition tells us that the world will be consumed by fire and there is no shortage of fire in these messages. But before the fire of Fatima there is also the purifying water of Lourdes. It is available to all who thirst and this should not be overlooked.

Centuries ago, the Blessed Virgin appeared to Saint Dominic and told him, "One day, through the power of the Rosary, I will save the world." Sister Lucia, in her interview with Father Fuentes, says that that time is now. She told Father Fuentes, "(The Blessed Virgin) made me understand... that we are in the last times of the world... God is giving two last remedies to the world. These are the Holy Rosary and Devotion to the Immaculate Heart of Mary. These are the last two remedies, which signify that there will be no others."[1] At Fatima the children were told to pray the Rosary every day. At Lourdes the Blessed Virgin carried a Rosary and at Akita Sister Agnes was told to pray the Rosary daily as well.

The faithful then, wait in hopeful expectation for the coming triumph of the Immaculate Heart. They await the day when the world is given, undeservedly, an era of peace. A truly Catholic peace. They await the triumph of the Virgin of Quito, La Salette and Fatima. They await the triumph of the Virgin of the Apocalypse.

---

1. *Sister Lucia – Apostle of Mary's Immaculate Heart,* p. 266.

# Postscript

<u>The Father Fuentes Interview</u>
  - Immense Spiritual and Physical Chastisements
  - Nations Wiped off the Face of the Earth
  - Satan Seduces Many Consecrated Religious Souls

What follows is the Father Fuentes interview. It does not mention specifics but simply restates the ongoing theme of the apparitions and the locution of Pope Leo XIII, i.e. that a war against, and the apostasy of, religious souls is taking place. In addition to the spiritual chastisement engulfing the Church, Sister Lucia refers to the material chastisements facing society as well. The interview was given in 1957, three years before the '3rd Secret of Fatima' was to be released by the Pope.

Fr. Fuentes: "I met her in her convent. She was very sad, very pale and emaciated. She said to me,

Sister Lucy: "Father, the most Holy Virgin is very sad because no one has paid any attention to Her Message, neither the good nor the bad. The good continue on their way, but without giving any importance to Her Message. The bad, not seeing the punishment of God actually falling upon them, continue their life of sin without even caring about the Message. But believe me, Father, God will chastise the world and this will be in a terrible manner. The punishment from Heaven is imminent. Father, how much time is there before 1960 arrives? It will be very sad for everyone, not one person will rejoice at all if beforehand the world does not pray and do penance.

I am not able to give any other details, because it is still a Secret. According to the will of the Most Holy Virgin, only the Holy Father and the Bishop of Fatima are permitted to know the Secret, but they have chosen to not know it so that they would not be influenced.

57

'...Tell them, Father, that many times the Most Holy Virgin told my cousins Francisco and Jacinta, as well as myself, that many nations will disappear from the face of the earth. She said that Russia will be the instrument of chastisement chosen by Heaven to punish the whole world if we do not beforehand obtain the conversion of that poor nation."

Fr. Fuentes: "Sister Lucy also told me, "Father, the devil is in the mood for engaging in a decisive battle against the Blessed Virgin. And the devil knows what it is that offends God the most, and which in a short space of time will gain for him the greatest number of souls. Thus the devil does everything to overcome souls consecrated to God, because in this way the devil will succeed in leaving the souls of the faithful abandoned by their leaders, thereby the more easily will he seize them. That which afflicts the Immaculate Heart of Mary and the Heart of Jesus is the fall of religious and priestly souls. The devil knows that religious and priests who fall away from their beautiful vocation drag numerous souls to hell.

...The devil wishes to take possession of consecrated souls. He tries to corrupt them in order to lull to sleep the souls of laypeople and thereby lead them to final impenitence. He employs all tricks, even going so far as to suggest the delay of entrance into religious life. Resulting from this is the sterility of the interior life, and among the laypeople, coldness (lack of enthusiasm) regarding the subject of renouncing pleasures and the total dedication of themselves to God. Tell them also, Father, that my cousins Francisco and Jacinta sacrificed themselves because in all the apparitions of the Most Holy Virgin, they always saw Her very sad. She never smiled at us. This sadness, this anguish which we noted in Her, penetrated our souls. This sadness is caused by the offenses against God and the punishments which menace sinners. And so, we children did not know what to think except to invent various means of praying and making sacrifices.

Father, that is why my mission is not to indicate to the world the material punishments which are certain to come if the world does not pray and do penance beforehand. No! My mission is to indicate to everyone the imminent danger we are in of losing our souls for all eternity if we remain obstinate in sin.

Fr. Fuentes: "Sister Lucy also said to me: "Father, we should not wait for an appeal to the world to come from Rome on the part of the Holy Father, to do penance. Nor should we wait for the call to penance to come from our bishops in our diocese, nor from the religious congregations. No! Our Lord has already very often used these means, and the world has not paid attention. That is why now, it is necessary for each one of us to begin to reform himself spiritually. Each person must not only save his own soul but also help to save all the souls that God has placed on our path. The devil does all in his power to distract us and to take away from us the love for prayer; we shall be saved together or we shall be damned together.

Father, the Most Holy Virgin did not tell me that we are in the last times of the world, but She made me understand this for three reasons. The first reason is because She told me that the devil is in the mood for engaging in a decisive battle against the Virgin. And a decisive battle is the final battle where one side will be victorious and the other side will suffer defeat. Also, from now on we must choose sides. Either we are for God or we are for the devil. There is no other possibility. The second reason is because She said to my cousins as well as to myself, that God is giving two last remedies to the world. These are the Holy Rosary and devotion to the Immaculate Heart of Mary. These are the last two remedies which signify that there will be no others.

The third reason is because in the plans of Divine Providence, God always, before He is about to chastise the world, exhausts all other remedies. Now, when He sees that the world pays no attention whatsoever, then as we say in our imperfect manner of speaking, He offers us with 'certain fear' the last means of salvation, His Most Holy Mother. It is with 'certain fear' because if you despise and repulse this ultimate means, we will not have any more forgiveness from Heaven, because we will have committed a sin which the Gospel calls the sin against the Holy Ghost. This sin consists of openly rejecting, with full knowledge and consent, the salvation which He offers. Let us remember that Jesus Christ is a very good Son and that He does not permit that we offend and despise His Most Holy Mother. We have recorded through many centuries of Church history the obvious testimony which demonstrates by the terrible chastisements which have befallen those who have attacked the honor of His Most Holy Mother, how Our Lord Jesus Christ has

59

always defended the honor of His Mother. The two means for saving the world are prayer and sacrifice.

Look, Father, the Most Holy Virgin, in these last times in which we live, has given a new efficacy to the recitation of the Rosary. She has given this efficacy to such an extent that there is no problem, no matter how difficult it is, whether temporal or above all spiritual, in the personal life of each one of us, of our families, of the families of the world or of the religious communities, or even of the life of peoples and nations, that cannot be solved by the Rosary. There is no problem I tell you, no matter how difficult it is, that we cannot resolve by the prayer of the Holy Rosary. With the Holy Rosary we will save ourselves. We will sanctify ourselves. We will console Our Lord and obtain the salvation of many souls.

Finally, devotion to the Immaculate Heart of Mary, our Most Holy Mother, consists in considering Her as the seat of mercy, of goodness and of pardon, and as the sure door by which we are to enter Heaven.[1]

The Prayers of Fatima
 - Saint Michael and the Virgin Demand Reparation

# The Fatima Prayers

Before teaching them the new prayers, Saint Michael told the children,

Offer prayers and sacrifices continually to the Most High. ...Make of everything you can a sacrifice, and offer it to God as an act of reparation for the sins by which He is offended, and in supplication for the conversion of sinners. ...Above all, accept and bear with submission the sufferings which the Lord will send you."

Likewise, the Blessed Virgin said, "Many souls go to Hell because there are none to sacrifice themselves and to pray for them."[2] Following these demands for reparation, they recited the following prayers unceasingly.

---

1. *Sister Lucia – Apostle of Mary's Immaculate Heart,* pp. 264-267.

2. http://www.theotokos.org.uk/pages/approved/words/wordfati.html

MY GOD, I believe, I adore, I hope and I love Thee and I implore Thy pardon for those who do not believe, do not adore, do not hope and do not love Thee!

MOST HOLY TRINITY, I adore Thee! My God, My God, I love Thee in the Most Holy Sacrament of the Altar!

MOST HOLY TRINITY, Father, Son and Holy Ghost, I adore Thee profoundly and I offer Thee the Most Precious Body, Blood, Soul and Divinity of Jesus Christ, Present in all the tabernacles of the earth. And in reparation for the outrages, sacrileges and indifference by which He, Himself is offended, and by the infinite merits of His Most Sacred Heart, and of the Immaculate Heart of Mary, I beg of Thee the conversion of poor sinners.

OH, MY JESUS, forgive us our sins and save us from the fires of Hell. Lead all souls to Heaven, especially those in most need.

OH, MY JESUS, it is for love of Thee, for the conversion of sinners, and in reparation for the sins committed against the Immaculate Heart of Mary... (that I offer up this sacrifice of _____).

The First Five Saturdays Devotion
- Devotion to the Immaculate Heart is God's Final Offer to Mankind

## The First Five Saturdays Devotion

On December 10, 1925, the Blessed Virgin appeared to Sister Lucia at her convent in Tuy, Spain. With her was the Child Jesus. As the Blessed Virgin held out her Immaculate Heart the Child Jesus said, "Have pity on this very sweet Heart which is continually martyred because of the ingratitude of men and has no one to console it with acts of reparation." Then the Blessed Virgin said,

> Look, my daughter, at my Heart encircled by these thorns with which men pierce it at every moment by their blasphemies and their ingratitude. Do you, at least, try to console me, and announce: I promise to assist at the hour of death with the grace necessary for salvation all those who, with the intention of making reparation to

me will, on the first Saturday of five consecutive months, go to confession, receive Holy Communion, say five decades of the beads, and keep me company for fifteen minutes while meditating on the fifteen mysteries of the rosary.[3]

As previously stated, during the apparitions of Fatima the Virgin had also said, "To those who embrace it, I promise salvation. These souls will be loved by God like flowers placed by me to adorn His throne."

*Sister Lucia's vision at Tuy, Spain, represents the Fatima message in its entirety: graces and mercy are offered with the worship of the Trinity and the Eucharist. Devotion/reparation to the Immaculate Heart of Mary is the last remedy being offered to the world.*

---

3. *The Sun Danced at Fatima,* p. 156.

Eternal salvation is promised to every soul who does the four simple tasks requested by the First Five Saturdays Devotion. With all the time that gets wasted surfing the internet, watching television and devoting energy to other tasks, who can argue that this is too much to ask?

## The Apparitions 'Score Sheet'

The following list is a tally sheet which lends definitive support to the veracity of the apparitions. In this mix we have a stigmatist, several incorruptibles, weeping statues and more. It also gives credence then, to the visionaries themselves.

The Ominous Date of October 13th:
Pope Leo XIII – Locution announcing Satan's unmitigated assault against the Church and her clergy thirty-three years to the day before the Fatima miracle.
The Miracle of the Sun – Witnessed by 70,000 at Fatima, Portugal.
Sister Agnes at Akita – Is given a message saying that much of mankind will be wiped out when fire falls from the sky.

The Incorruptibles:
Venerable Mother Mariana
Saint Catherine Laboure
Saint Bernadette
Saint Don Bosco
Blessed Jacinta Marto

One Stigmatist and a Weeping, Sweating, Wooden Stigmatized Statue
Sister Agnes Sasagawa of Akita

Severe Spiritual and Physical Chastisements
Quito
La Salette
Fatima
Akita
Pope Leo XIII
Pope John Paul II

Apostasy, the Antichrist and St. Michael the Archangel
Quito
La Salette
Fatima
Cardinal Oddi
Cardinal Ratzinger
Pope John Paul II

The 'End Times'
La Salette
Fatima
Cardinal Ratzinger
Pope John Paul II
Sister Lucia
Scripture

Martyrdom of Pope, Clergy and Faithful
La Salette
Fatima
Saint Don Bosco
Pope John Paul II

Too Scary to Even Release It:
Cardinal Ratzinger
Pope John Paul II

The Rosary and Devotion to the Immaculate Heart is the Answer
Saint Dominic
Lourdes
Fatima
Akita
Sister Lucia
Pope John Paul II

# Bibliography

Brother Michel de la Sainte Trinité, *The Whole Truth About Fatima,* Volume III, "The Third Secret". Immaculate Heart Publications, Buffalo, New York, 1990.

Fellows, Mark, *Sister Lucia – Apostle of Mary's Immaculate Heart,* Immaculate Heart Publications, Buffalo, New York, 2007.

Ferrara, Christopher A., *The Secret Still Hidden,* Good Counsel Publications, Pound Ridge, New York, 2008.

Horvat, Ph. D, Marian Therese, *Our Lady of Good Success – Prophecies For Our Times,* Tradition in Action, Inc., Los Angeles, California, 1999.

Kramer, Father Paul, *The Devil's Final Battle.* The Missionary Association, Terryville, Connecticut, 2002.

Pelletier, Joseph A., A.A., *The Sun Danced at Fatima,* An Image Book, New York, New York, 1983.

*Secrets of La Salette,* The 101 Foundation, Asbury, New Jersey, 1994.

Yasuda, Father Teiji, *Akita – The Tears and Message of Mary,* The 101 Foundation, Asbury, New Jersey, 1989.

# **Notes**

Made in the USA
San Bernardino, CA
28 April 2014